THE OFFICIAL SUMMARY OF

RISING TO POWER

THE JOURNEY OF EXCEPTIONAL EXECUTIVES

by Ron A. Carucci & Eric C. Hansen

MAIN IDEA PRESS

Published by Main Idea Press
Austin, TX
www.greenleafbookgroup.com

Distributed by Main Idea Press

Design and composition by Greenleaf Book Group
Cover design by Greenleaf Book Group

Print ISBN: 978-0-9980112-2-6

eBook ISBN: 978-0-9980112-3-3

First Edition

CONTENTS

SYNOPSIS

Nearly two-thirds of all leaders entering into executive roles lack sufficient understanding of what is required of them and are underprepared for what they will face, which explains why fifty percent of them fail within the first eighteen months.

Rising to Power acknowledges the gap between a new executive's understanding and their abilities, seeking to guide readers through their ascent, transitional moments, and identification of the common issues that may arise for new executives promotions once they acclimate to the job.

Carucci and Hansen have decades of experience consulting in business management and executive leadership. In writing their book, the authors performed a ten-year longitudinal study of executive promotions and assessed many organizations and their leaders to identify why some fail and others succeeded.

They found that many of the issues newly minted executives face are a result of rising to leadership roles earlier than ever, despite a lack of experience and after minimal—if any—formal development. As a result of these deficiencies, many of these new executives become paralyzed and are unable to make actionable decisions or let go of their previous responsibilities. They become unable to affect performance and eventually fail. If you're an executive—or you're aspiring to be one—this book is an excellent resource.

Rising to Power is divided into four sections that chart different challenges executives face in their journey to success: *Ascend, Adjust, Assert*, and *Affect*.

Ascend details executive preparation as an evolutionary journey, not just a series of disparate and disconnected events. It explains that the initial shock and disorientation executives feel when entering their new roles ("altitude sickness") to the top of their corporate hierarchy is caused by a lack of mental and emotional preparedness. It takes time to acclimatize to the new perspective and responsibilities their job requires. The authors write that by assessing the needs and different "altitudes" of the organization and identifying your part in your organization, you can avoid the debilitating effects of altitude sickness.

Adjust addresses how to be intentional about the transition into your new role by carefully planning your exit from your previous work. This process will cement you into your organization's strategic system. Carucci and Hansen stress that every executive should have a plan, whether they are arriving from outside an organization or within it, about how they will successfully integrate into their new role. The authors also caution readers that they need to identify any distorted perspectives that could keep them from clearly assessing their position and the actions they need to take to be successful.

Assert instructs readers in how they can effectively balance the exercise of positional, relational, and informational power and carefully manage the expectations of their employees. Carucci and Hansen tell readers they can use their new executive power effectively without abusing it if they focus on three power sources: positional, relational, and informational. Perversions of these powers are common, yet avoidable. The chapter advises readers on how to identify and overcome these abuses. This section also guides executives through managing expectations now that they are in a position of power. Frequently, executives fall short of the many different expectations that come from their employees, their C-suite colleagues, and themselves, and they fail to identify what is *really* being expected from them.

Finally, *Affect* examines the lasting impact that effective leaders can have on an organization. Through their collective research, the authors give a blueprint for the four capabilities that exceptional executives consistently display: breadth, context, choice, and connection.

Most executives fail because they are unprepared for the job. It may be their own misunderstanding of the expectations of their position, or a failure of their organization to communicate the realities of a leadership role. *Rising to Power* helps ascending executives navigate these predictable difficulties. Ron Carucci and Eric Hansen have crafted an in-depth and detailed guide through the tough transitional moments that may arise in your executive ascent. *Rising to Power* offers a profoundly new way of looking at this journey and offers real approaches to significantly increase your chances of success.

Introduction—Wing Walking: An Executive's Sudden Rise to Power

Main Ideas

- A "rising" journey within an organization is not a linear process. Rather, the path to being an exceptional executive is more indirect with a variety of experiences that spur growth.
- The life of an executive balances moments of struggle and accomplishment.

Key Concepts

Transition: not a one-time event, rather an ongoing adaptation of one's leadership behaviors to the context of circumstances one leads in.

Summary

Many executives take the reins of leadership before they are ready. These executives find themselves unable to let go of the security their previous position offered them and move forward into their full responsibilities, ultimately failing to complete their executive journey.

This inertia may come from a major flaw in the beliefs surrounding the executive's rising journey: that the process is linear. *Rising to Power* teaches the important lesson that *transitioning* is not a one-time event or a simple, direct sequence of promotions. Executive preparation and performance must be viewed as one continuous journey with predictable phases, each of which has addressable challenges that, if viewed collectively, more holistically and sustainably prepare executives to assume increasingly broader levels of responsibility.

There are seven factors found to influence the success or failure of transitioning executives: having faulty assumptions or incorrect expectations about their role; being afraid of challenges to the status quo; being challenged by new coworkers; and having the revelation that they lack the ability to lead.

Exceptional executives have many components: the ability to learn, an understanding of business systems, emotional intelligence, character, and clear aspirations. Though these individual qualities are important, it's how they fit together with each other that makes executives noteworthy.

Successful executive leadership inherently includes pain and privilege. These experiences provide a necessary crucible that forges effective executives. Those who can successfully balance the dual nature of their role are those who desire to make a difference. Leaders affect lives. The higher you rise, the more lives you can positively impact. If your rise to power has meaning and you understand how your leadership affects others, you have a much higher chance of success.

Important Quote

"Prepared or not, organizations are placing bets on younger leaders in an attempt to achieve better strategic results. And with opportunity coming well in advance of the experience, knowledge, and relational and emotional maturity necessary to sustain success, failure rates are astounding but predictable." (1-2)

SECTION I: ASCEND

Chapter 1—Altitude Sickness: Acclimatizing to the Realities of Executive Leadership

Main Ideas

- People who rise to executive roles have often idealized the job. When the realities of the executive position become apparent, people often experience "summit shock."
- Frustrating transitional periods are normal.

Key Concepts

Summit Shock: The uncertainty that arises when an executive's expectations of a role conflict with the actual day-to-day duties of the job or when they outpace their skill level.

Idealization: A cognitive-emotional process that calms your anxieties and steels your confidence to move forward with a decision by focusing on, reinforcing, and even exaggerating the positive qualities and potential of your choices.

Cognitive Dissonance: The uncomfortable tension that arises when our beliefs, behaviors, or attitudes conflict with the world around us.

Summary

Summit shock, or altitude sickness, usually occurs when people climb to high altitudes without giving their bodies proper time to adjust to the lower levels of oxygen in the atmosphere. Executives who rise very quickly to the top of their organizations also experience similarly debilitating and disorienting symptoms. Many have *idealized* their new role and are caught off-guard by their new day-to-day reality.

A rise to power will always include change and uncertainty. A healthy questioning of your abilities, when harnessed positively, can sharpen your learning edge, heighten energy levels, and elevate effectiveness. However, if self-doubt festers, it can turn into self-destructive behaviors. Our brains trigger irrational ideas to eliminate the clash in our beliefs about the reality of this new world and ourselves, a damaging behavior referred to as *cognitive dissonance*.

The shock you experience in this transitional period is normal. Effective leaders must work to resolve the reality of their situation from their idealized version and get through their *summit shock*.

Effective acclimatization demands awareness of the story you tell yourself about your rise so that you may shift focus to what is needed by the organization and accurately assess what you can do in your role. Increase your perspective and identify what the needs of your organization are and its context before making decisions. Success comes from reflecting and understanding a situation before deciding how to act. Understanding the many layers of your organization will help you identify how your position provides you the opportunity to offer unique solutions based on your elevated perspective.

You must also resist relying on the history of your accomplishments rather than creating a new vision for the future. Your rise does not supply you with a mandate; rather, you have been given an opportunity to improve yourself and your company. Applying past solutions to new problems does not usually work. The role of an executive is to critically assess the current situation, adapt knowledge, and take calculated actions to impact the company in years to come. Executives must learn to think and react in the long term.

Essential Takeaways

- Proactively anticipate and address the symptoms of "altitude sickness" and acclimatize to higher altitudes; manage "summit shock."
- Resist the "myth of the mandate" that you have been brought in just to make specific changes.

Important Quote

"As you arrive at the next career summit, an important first shift is to consciously assess the stories you are telling yourself about why and how you got here. This is vital because how you think about yourself in your new role will trigger the behaviors by which you'll be judged and that will ultimately drive your success or failure." (34)

Chapter 2—Distinguishing Your Organization's Different Altitudes: Transitioning to the Strategic System

Main Ideas

- When well-intended executives are over-involved in the departments or positions they've left behind, they fail to support the company's future.
- Executives need a mental shift to fully adjust.
- Successful organizations are made of three interdependent systems: operating, coordinating, and strategic.

Key Concepts

The Operating System: The people and processes that transform inputs and deliver finished goods and services to the market. It is central.

The Coordinating System: The people who oversee the Operating system and know how to collaborate across the organization to get things done.

The Strategic System: The people who work on designing and refining all three systems.

Summary

There are three distinct, interdependent structural systems of every successful organization: the *Operating system*, the *Coordinating system*, and the *Strategic system*.

There are challenges associated with the executive's transition into the *Strategic System*. The Strategic system works on the system of the organization itself. Roles falling within the Strategic system are primarily responsible for monitoring external trends, defining the company's competitive position, securing and allocating capital, defining corporate values, defining and evolving the organization as needed, and developing senior enterprise talent.

Members of the Strategic system must under go a mental shift about how they defining value-adding work to effectively contribute. The main role of an executive is to set the direction of the company. Working on the system itself requires finding your role in the system. You have to assess how the systems do (or don't) achieve desired results. It is your responsibility to maintain a broad understanding of the organization and not get bogged down in the day-to-day operations. That is what the Coordinating system is there to do.

The Coordinating system is primarily responsible for four main areas. First, they translate strategy into day-to-day work. Next, they manage resources and assign them to be used where there is the highest probability of success.

They are also responsible for increasing and transferring the knowledge and skills of the Operating system to developing talents. Lastly, this system is responsible for reinforcing the operating philosophy of the company and enacting its desired culture.

Leaders in the Strategic system must trust the leaders in the Coordinating system to solve issues that arise. Their job is to support and make sure they understand strategy in the right context. It is important to judge when there is an issue in understanding strategy that necessitates stepping in, and when to let things go.

Understand the scale of your position. Your words have impact. In the Strategic system, you are no longer just a manager, but a leader. Your words and actions impact the lives of the company and its people. Your success and the success of the people you lead depends on your conscious choice to play at the level your organization needs.

Essential Takeaways

- See current and future roles in the context of the entirety of an organization—as an executive, transition from the Coordinating system to the Strategic system.
- Identify and differentiate the expectations at each altitude; consciously contribute to both the technical and leadership expectations of each role.

Important Quote

"When leaders work at the wrong level, the substantive work needed in support of the future doesn't get done. Talent doesn't get developed, innovation doesn't thrive, the performance culture doesn't get strengthened, and over time the business starts to run out of ways to grow organically and sustainably." (48-49)

SECTION II: ADJUST

Chapter 3—Planning Your Shift to the Strategic System: Separating from What You Left Behind

Main Ideas

- A well-executed entry strategy requires you to think like an anthropologist. You will need a learning plan.
- Your arrival plan should be adapted to your situation.
- You will need to shift your mindset so that you're able to use the information you have learned about your company most effectively.

Key Concepts

Moving in: Executives who obtain leadership positions from outside the company.

Moving up: Executives who rise to leadership positions from within the company.

Anthropologist: An executive who begins his shift into the Strategic system by digging in, learning about the organization with open-mindedness, and identifying its real culture, issues, and opportunities.

Summary

Sixty-seven percent of executives struggle to let go of the work of their previous roles. However, they lament the time spent dealing with the performance shortfalls of others.

Executives must plan for their shift to the Strategic system. Whether they obtain an executive role from inside an organization or outside, effective executives must begin with an anthropologist's mindset: ready to discard preconceived hypotheses about the organization and actively learn about it and its people.

The anthropological dig into the organization comes as part of creating a plan for entering the Strategic system. While forming your plan, gather disconfirming data in order to provide "checks and balances" of your predisposed assumptions about the organization. This breadth of data may contain key information and opportunities that you may not be naturally inclined to seek. Sift through it, identifying patterns that identify vital priorities that you can align the organization toward achieving.

It is difficult to inherit a predecessor's team—you need to build your own. Identify the right talent that works best with you and will help move the organization in the direction you want to take it. As you work with these new people, stay conscious of the verbal and non-verbal messages you are sending them. Seek their feedback and act upon it rather than assuming your intentions are clearly conveyed.

In addition, if you are entering the Strategic system from outside the company, seek to establish authentic relationships so that people get to know, trust, and respect you. You should also be mindful of your diagnosis of the current situation. Make any criticisms judiciously and constructively.

If you are rising to an executive role from within a company, there are extra challenges to consider. You need to adjust relationships with peers and direct reports. They need to know that you are still the same person they knew before, but the ways you relate to each other and interact need to change.

Abandon any biases you have about the organization. Your previous knowledge can provide insight, but these preconceptions can impede moving the company forward if they distort the perspective needed in your new role. Strive to see the whole of the organization, rather than focusing on just the familiar. When you encounter problems, diagnose them without indictment.

Similarly, you should avoid doing any work from your previous roles in the Coordinating system. Letting go of the responsibilities of previous roles and shifting to the mindset of the Strategic system is a struggle for most executives. Leaders often find it difficult to allow workers to do things their way rather than stepping in and micromanaging at the lower levels. You should remove yourself completely and leave it to the new people to handle, even if they aren't one hundred percent ready. Executives are there to give direction, not execute.

Weak executives often react immediately to fix a problem rather than stepping back and assessing future outcomes. As an executive, you need a broad view of what the organization needs rather than just seeing its individual parts.

Many executives struggle with time allocation. In the Strategic system, you have to pick your battles. It is important to identify which demands require personal action and which should be delegated. Proper delegation will free up your time and allow others to develop the confidence to make decisions without your input.

Essential Takeaways

- Anticipate and practice letting go of the aspects of your current job ahead of the timeframe for your next transition.
- Build a learning plan that first targets gathering disconfirming data.
- Synthesize learning into a shared set of "vital few" priorities.
- Size up talent and build your team.
- Build authentic relationships (vertical and horizontal); allow people to get to know you.

- Blend into your new role without "going native" and losing your fresh perspective.
- See the whole; diagnose without indicting.
- Solicit and act upon personal feedback at key intervals.

Important Quote

"An effective executive enters the Strategic system as a true anthropologist—setting aside preconceived hypotheses about what she will discover and genuinely seeking to 'learn' the organization and its people." (68)

Chapter 4—Altitudinal Distortions: How You and the World Look Different from Up Here

Main Ideas

- How others see and relate to you changes significantly as you rise; distortions of you get created.
- Having keen perception of oneself and one's role helps executives see through the distorted views of others.
- Effective executives can identify historical, horizontal, economic, and cultural patterns within their organization and marketplace to inform critical decisions.

Key Concepts

Operative Narrative: The story that a newly risen executive tells himself about his professional journey and the reasons for it.

Distortions: The altered or unnatural perceptions that people have of you once you have taken an elevated position in your company, such as *Larger than Life*, *The Megaphone Effect*, *Sifted Data*, and *Aliens Next Door*.

Pattern: A consistent or reliable collection of traits, tendencies, or other observable characteristics that an executive must perceive; can be historical, horizontal, economical, and cultural.

Summary

As you rise, how others see and relate to you changes significantly. Many newly promoted people find that their new status comes with several distortions that leave them feeling off balance.

Sixty percent of executives struggle with the realization that others ascribe more power to them than they actually believe they have. The *Larger than Life* distortion happens when you come to embody a company or product. People define you in an exaggerated fashion in the context of the position you hold. It is necessary to take steps to prevent a default persona from becoming the way people see you. Be thoughtful about how accessible you are, and when necessary, take steps to increase that access with key individuals or groups. By providing insights to who you are and what you believe, as your influence grows, you will be more successful in forming your intended image. The higher up you are, the more your reputation matters. You won't be able to control everything people believe, but if you are not deliberate about what others see and how people experience you, chances are the image they form will be distorted.

The *Megaphone Effect* occurs when your behavioral and

verbal messages become amplified with your elevated status. When you are one of the top leaders in your organization, there is no "small talk." Try to be as clear as you can about your intentions and as precise as possible in your communication, a process we call "leading out loud."

Sifted data occurs when the quality and quantity of data shared with an executive is sanitized. To combat this distortion, take stock of how information flows within your business. Regardless of your personal style, how information comes to your level is largely influenced by a broader set of historic assumptions already in play. Information is a currency of influence; identify the key power brokers and establish a relationship with them. Find opportunities early and often to prove to your organization that you are trustworthy and able to handle to truth, that you won't "shoot the messenger" but rather welcome even bad news.

The *Aliens Next Door* distortion happens when new leaders experience a change in interactions with peers and direct reports that results in alienation from formerly comfortable relationships. Although you probably haven't changed as a person, your responsibilities have. As such, effective executives redefine expectations and boundaries of their existing relationships with colleagues who have become their direct reports and peers.

Alienation can leave an executive feeling isolated and anxious, leading to hasty decisions in order to be liked and accepted. The best way to gain confidence and bridge the gaps in your relationships is through thoughtful interactions with peers and direct reports. Decide what kind of executive you are going to be, what actions you are going to take, and understand how others will see each decision you make and form an opinion about you because of it.

One of the biggest challenges to overcoming altitudinal distortions can be accurately identifying your *operative narrative*, or the stories that you tell yourself about your situation, how others perceive you, and your strengths and weaknesses. A successful executive understands and manages their operative narratives and triggers. Managing self-perception, skills, and insecurities while acknowledging destructive behaviors is necessary for your executive success. Our triggers generate our unconscious reflective responses to situations. Knowing the narrative underneath those triggers helps you modify those reactions to more productive choices.

At this point in your career and life, you have been shaped by multitudinous forces, experiences, and challenges that have created a foundation of beliefs and values. This system of beliefs is what defines your individuality. Hold tight to it in the face of all these distortions.

Knowing oneself also includes knowing one's weaknesses. As you rise in an organization, personal problems become potential professional disasters. Do the deeper work necessary to confront what, to this point, you have learned to contain. Discover, decode, and redo any destructive or misguided narratives you have about yourself or your rise. Do not fear criticism. Let your team know that they have your permission to provide you feedback, and thank them profusely.

After you have done the work to strengthen your identity and fight your fears, and have given permission for feedback, you can address organizational distortions by creating positive partnerships to anchor yourself and shift from being a problem solver to a pattern recognizer. In the Strategic system it is important to see *patterns* in the marketplace, in how the organization responds, how groups function, and how people behave. There are four main types of patterns that effective leaders find most beneficial to evaluate and respond to: *historical, horizontal, economic,* and *cultural.*

Analyzing historical patterns helps determine how well an organization will perform in the future; while isolated events are less effective in determining direction. Horizontal patterns are common things seen across all aspects of the company that may or may not be healthy. Understanding true horizontal patterns, like risk aversion or excessive consensus seeking, is difficult. Many executives make the mistake of over-relying on anecdotes and hyperbole rather than assessing what the true patterns are.

Economic patterns come from analyzing an array of financial data sets, including sales trends, costs, margins, ROICs, cash reserves, industry and geographic buying patterns, and commodity costs, in order to identify emerging patterns of significance. Translating these patterns into actions creates competitive differentiation and keeps unwanted costs down as demand gets created.

Cultural patterns are identified by amassing surveys and collected data to evaluate the emotional health and engagement of an organization's employees. Identifying these patterns can help executives shift focus and keep people engaged and achieve optimal performance from them.

Essential Takeaways

- Identify the operative narratives that shape your behavior.
- Make time for intentional reflection.
- Create and anchor yourself to positive partnerships; have climbing partners to assist you during and after your transition.
- Detect patterns to clear up organizational distortions.
- Take the time to think before you say or do anything.
- Help others adjust their own distortions.

Important Quote

"It won't be any one spectacular event that secures your rise to power. It will be the way you transact your business and relationships—one consistent interaction, trade-off, apology, challenge, and high-five after another. Executive credibility is built on the day-to-day experiences of your leadership." (115)

SECTION III: ASSERT

Chapter 5—Executive Power: Perversions, Abuses, and the Greater Good

Main Ideas

- Executive power plays an important role in effective leadership based on how it is dispensed and the perceptions and experiences of those on either end of the power dynamic.
- It is difficult to balance exerting power over others and power in service of others. Abuses and perversions of power lead to failure of executives.
- An effective executive can redeem executive power by casting aside self-interest and self-protection in favor of the greater good of the company.

Key Concepts

Positional Power: using your position of authority as a leader to serve others

Relational Power: The power that comes from the important relationships you hold and the influence you garner because of those relationships

Informational Power: Using either hard data or the interpretation of such to influence others; using responsible access to especially privileged or confidential information

Summary

For executives, power abuses and perversions are common, but not inevitable. As an organization leader your impact on others and legacy in the company are largely contingent upon how you deploy the executive power that comes with your position.

The perceptions and experiences of those on either end of the power dynamic can shape an organization in dramatically different ways. Abuses—indulgent self-interest, and perversions—and abdication for self-protection are common and lead executives to fail.

There are three main sources of executive power: *Positional, Relational,* and *Informational.*

Positional power is an executive's ability to use the formal authority of their position to make decisions and exert influence over others. Perversions of Positional power, when individuals' agendas trump the enterprise's agenda, result in indecision, including paralysis, over-inclusion, accommodation, and the fear of making mistakes or disappointing others. Abuse of Positional power is formed by egoism, the belittling of others, and excessive self-interest.

Relational power is the influence you garner through the strength of connections. It could be access to especially powerful people, or garnering the loyalty of influential informal leaders. You can abuse Relational power if you exploit people to advance your own cause or bribe others by promising rewards in exchange for loyalty, political support, or compromising actions.

Perversions of Relational power are when people are counter-dependent and co-dependent—behaving as if either others don't matter to you and you don't need them or as if others are indispensable to you and you can't function without them.

Informational power comes from using data or its interpretation to wield influence. Some common forms of abuse of Informational power include intentionally twisting or withholding information to manipulate circumstances or threatening to use information to harm others. Perversions of Informational power include failing to listen to or control messaging that leads to confusion or carelessly divulging confidential information through "executive gossip."

These abuses and perversions are avoidable. Positional power can be redeemed using justice and meritocracy to build confidence and trust. People in an organization want to know that their contributions matter and be rewarded fairly. There may be long-standing notions of injustice and tolerating poor performance prior to a new executive's arrival. Break that cycle and take the time to reverse any inherited notions of injustice and rationalizations about performance.

Redeeming Relational power lies in the positive regard and personal investment you make in others by shaping relationships grounded in commitment and sacrifice. An effective executive can redeem executive power by casting aside self-interest and self-protection in favor of the greater good of the company and doing what is right despite the risk of facing criticism.

The abuses and perversions of Informational power can be redeemed with knowledge and transparency. Two things happen when people feel they have adequate access to information they need to do their jobs as well as the reasons behind decisions made: they learn the value of their work and are inspired to work more and work better with others.

Essential Takeaways

- Understand both the abuses and perversions of organizational power, and where you may susceptible to either.
- Use your own behaviors to set the standards for others and take responsibility if you fall short of them yourself.
- Lead an equitable organization and use your power to right any injustices.
- Share information in ways that make your decision making process transparent.

- Build relationships with those you lead in ways that strengthen your knowledge of them so you can use that knowledge for their benefit.
- Share the privileges that accompany your role with those that wouldn't normally benefit from them.

Important Quote

"You can beat the odds of executive failure by becoming an honest, humble, diligent steward of your positional, relational, and informational power." (153-154)

Chapter 6—Managing Expectations: Translating Chronic Failure and Unrealistic Demands into Kept Promises

Main Ideas

- Executives struggle to live up to the unrealistic expectation of their direct reports.
- The unrealistic expectations are the result of widespread leadership failure
- Knowing how to interpret the underlying legitimate needs beneath the unrealistic expectations is the key to building credibility.

Key Concepts

Unrealistic Expectations: The exaggerated beliefs about and standards for executives that workers may have, such as *Perfection*, *Equity and Fairness*, *Transparency and Justification*, *Clairvoyance*, *Accessibility*, and *Inspiration*.

Summary

Managing *expectations* is a major obstacle to executive success. Whether entering from outside the company, or rising from within it, there will inevitably be a set of assumptions coming at you from all sides. The expectations from direct reports can be the most challenging to address.

Executives usually start out as untrusted and are burdened with both realistic and unrealistic expectations that keep them feeling off balance. The best way to manage unrealistic expectations is to identify what people really want and keep the appropriate promises to set healthy expectations.

Perfection is a common expectation with consequences. Overachieving executives who have no room for failure of any kind—morally, technically, or relationally—often alienate their followers by pursuing perfection, eventually training them to expect perfection.

The legitimate need that underlies this unrealistic demand is that direct reports expect leaders to perform at a higher standard of competence and principles. Executives should not hold others accountable to the standards they themselves are not willing or able to live up to and should take responsibility when they do fall short.

Equity and Fairness are an unrealistic demand that every decision a leader makes should be equally beneficial, with no one being treated unfairly. In reality, there should be a clear rationale about how rewards and resources are distributed. Executives need to be sure to treat everyone with "equity," which might not always mean equal. However, people must know their effort and results will be fairly evaluated and rewarded, and against what criteria.

People have formed an unrealistic demand for *Transparency and Justification* in leaders' decision-making process. People mistakenly believe they are entitled to leaders' every decision, especially when they are directly impacted by those decisions. People want to be able to predict what you will do and understand your motives so that they feel more comfortable working with you. You should act based on fact-based information and the thinking behind your decisions should be made clear, even if you do not share all of your information with your reports.

Direct reports often expect a certain level of *clairvoyance* from executives. Executives are expected to know when people are dissatisfied without being told. There are legitimate concerns buried in this expectation. People want to be seen for who they are and how well they work. Executives should get to know their workers as people to build trust among direct reports.

Accessibility is another expectation that has formed unrealistic demands over years of failed leadership. People believe executives should be available at any time of the day for anything. Executives shouldn't involve themselves in the organization's minutiae, but they should be as responsive as possible with the demands of the leadership role they are in and make clear the process for getting their time and attention.

Others also demand *Inspiration* from leaders. Direct reports expect executives to keep them feeling safe in their positions, energized, and encouraged to continue with their work. In reality, people just need to know that the work they do has meaning, and that there is a reason to hope in the face of challenging circumstances.

Essential Takeaways

- Anticipate follower expectations and work to build credibility by making and keeping commitments by—
    - Living up to the standards you set
    - Leading equitably, never promise "equality"; make right organizational injustices
    - Providing decision-making transparency
    - Being a student of those you lead—anticipation of needs through "knowing" them
    - Giving reasonable accessibility
    - Inspiring hope through personal passion and honest assessment of setbacks

Important Quote

"Anchoring yourself with a set of values that aren't vulnerable to the sometimes fickle, unpredictable needs of followers; knowing yourself well—your character, your strengths, your flat sides, your passions; and possessing a genuine desire to make a difference, not just for yourself but for the organization in which you lead, will help you weather the sometimes overly harsh blows dealt by followers through stringent and unrealistic expectations." (172)

SECTION IV: AFFECT

Chapter 7—The Exceptional Executive: Powerful Leadership in Action

Main Ideas

- Specific competencies revealed in the research play a major role in the effectiveness of executive leadership. Executives must demonstrate *Breadth*, *Choice*, *Context*, and *Connection* in order to successfully guide their organizations and inspire confidence from their people.
- When these are used in concert, optimal effectiveness is achieved.

Key Concepts

Breadth: The deep knowledge of how all the "pieces" of the organization fit together, the value they create in driving results, and how to integrate the organization's "seams" so that poor coordination, silos, and fragmentation turn into competitive performance.

Choice: The ability to assemble the right information and construct complex decisions and solutions with the right balance of data, input, intuition, and analysis. In addition to a well-defined process for making and communicating decisions, exceptional executives sustain a clear and consistent focus on the critical few choices that have to be made to avoid overwhelming the system with too many priorities, driving unity of purpose and enhancing the potential for success.

Context: Expert knowledge of the industry and marketplace dynamics in which the business competes, how it makes "money," keeping abreast of competitive and industry shifts and trends on the horizon, and adapting in advance of the need to. Deep knowledge of the unique competitive requirements of the organization to differentiate and win.

Connection: The ability to form deep, trust-based relationships with bosses, peers, and direct reports through consistent interaction based on trust, commitment, honesty, and respect. Exceptional executives maintain in-depth knowledge of all key stakeholders and their contributions. The ability to form healthy attachments generates successful outcomes with others.

Summary

The most effective executives are identified by consistent patterns of executive practice that directly enable sustained, positive impact on performance. They demonstrate mastery of the "big picture" by having an intimate, up-to-date understanding of economic and competitive marketplace dynamics and an understanding of how the business works. Top executives also have exceptionally strong knowledge of their business and the role and contributions of the organization they lead.

Successful executives also develop a network of relationships that deeply influence the skills needed to successfully execute enterprise-wide initiatives that have impact. They also seek ideas and opinions from different networks in order to incorporate them into plans to solve organizational problems to generate influence in all relationships.

Transparency is another distinguishing factor. Top executives rely on their own analytical skills along with the knowledge of others to come to decisions. This, as well as a balanced process of communication, awards them the trust and respect necessary to lead and produce results.

There are four key interdependent competencies synchronized as one that make up an exceptional executive: *Breadth*, *Context*, *Choice*, and *Connection*.

Without knowledge of the working parts of an organization and how they fit together into a cohesive whole, solving problems becomes more challenging. Executives tend to resolves issues in the *context* of their own expertise. This largely ignores the complexities of the system and, lacking a more comprehensive view of the organization, leaders often end up trying to solve mere symptoms rather than underlying problems. Leaders who develop a full understanding of the various parts of the organization and how they are meant to integrate will achieve greater success. The deeper an executive's understanding of the specific context of the position is, the deeper and more sustainable the impact their decisions will have. *Choice* is the ability to assemble the right information and construct complex decisions and solutions with the right balance of data, input from others, intuition, and analysis. Finally, *Connection* is an important source of executive capability.

These four dimensions generate maximum effectiveness when leveraged in concert with one another. Exceptional executives are distinguished by their understanding and effective development of these competencies as an integrated whole. As you assess and prioritize your development, maintain a balanced view of how they are all working together. An overemphasis in one may lead to deficiency in another. It is only when they are elegantly working in concert that you will be able to appreciate that their power, in part, emanates from their utter simplicity accompanied by their profound collective impact.

While these are not the only attributes of effective executives, the research showed that they overwhelmingly distinguished top performing leaders who are able to lead their organizations and achieve exceptional success. As you incorporate these dimensions into your practices, keep their simplicity in mind. Be patient with your process; there will be setbacks and each new role and altitude will have its challenges. Diligence is the price you pay for rising. Leading is a never-ending adaptation and a rewarding journey.

Essential Takeaways

- Consciously develop an understanding of the organization as a whole and actively exploit the knowledge of how the various parts work in concert to manage complexity and create value.
- Seek and apply intricate knowledge of your business to emerging competitive threats by constantly scanning and looking for trends, patterns, and emerging possibilities on a multi-year horizon.
- Hone your ability to identify and construct the choices needed for the organizations to advance. Develop a healthy balance of instinct and analysis, and consciously blend your ideas with the voices of others into focused choices that align others to a common direction and common priorities.
- Cultivate positive connections with stakeholders at all levels. Meet with them regularly and listen deeply to discover what motivates them and what their priorities are, as well as to understand the challenges they may be facing—especially at key points of intersection with your areas of responsibility to align on mutual direction and expectations.

Important Quote

"Only when leveraged in concert with one another can [these capabilities] generate maximum impact. It is in the understanding and effective development of them as an integrated whole that executives are enabled to truly rise to power." (209)

Epilogue—Controlled Burns: Committing to Your Rise by Leaving Behind What Got You Here to Create Something Exceptional.

Main Ideas

- Seventy percent of the American workforce is not engaged at work. Executive failure and distrust is a major contributor.
- Executives are responsible for transforming the workplace through hard work and sacrifice in order to make a significant difference.

Key Concept

Controlled Burning: a technique used for forest management by intentionally creating fires to lower the chance and severity of natural fires later. In organizational life this references examining and abandoning past practices and privileges that, although comfortable, can potentially be destructive.

Summary

The increasing reality of disenfranchised people in the workplace requires that executives must change how they lead in order to restore commitment and morale.

An estimated seventy percent of employees are not engaged at work. Much of this disinterest in work comes from an extreme distrust in leaders' motives and abilities.

Stories of executive abuse and excessive compensation are widespread; therefore, many workers have lost confidence in their organization. It is vital that executives internalize this reality and decide if they can and/or should make a difference when ascending to their position.

To make a difference, leaders need to make sacrifices. This practice is analogous to the idea of *controlled burning*. A controlled burn is a forest management technique where fires are intentionally set and controlled in order to alleviate the severity of natural fires in the future.

The same principle applies to executives. In order to flourish, leaders must execute their own controlled burns targeting privileges, experiences, practices, accolades, relationships, beliefs, behaviors, skills, and other aspects of their career that have accompanied their rise to power. These, although comfortable and useful in their previous context, may be destructive to a new role. A controlled burn can be large or small, and cleansing these comforts and rewards in order to benefit the greater good can be difficult. However, taking this leap of faith will lead to better harnessing the power of Context, enhancing Breadth, mastering the power of Choice, and deepening Connection.

Important Quote

"Throughout your rise, you must believe you can and should leave your part of the world better than you found it. To do so, you must burn off anything that could thwart your rise for the sake of creating something exceptional." [237]

ABOUT THE AUTHORS

Ron A. Carucci, managing partner at Navalent, is a seasoned consultant with more than twenty-five years of experience working with CEOs and senior executives of organizations ranging from Fortune 50 to start-ups in pursuit of transformational change. He has taught at the graduate school level and is the author of seven other books, including the acclaimed *Leadership Divided: What Emerging Leaders Need and What You Might Be Missing*. He is a regular contributor to *Forbes* and *Harvard Business Review*. His work has been featured in *Fortune*, *CEO Magazine*, *Inc.*, *BusinessInsider*, MSNBC, and *Business Week*.

Eric C. Hansen, managing partner at Navalent, has thirty years of business management, executive leadership, and consulting experience, having worked for the May Company, Intel Corporation, AT&T Capital Corporation, Hallmark Cards Inc., and the Abu Dhabi Investment Authority. He holds an undergraduate degree in business and a master's degree in organizational behavior from Brigham Young University.

Made in United States
Orlando, FL
23 January 2024

42819846R10029